Sing of Jesus, son of Mary,
In the home of Nazareth.
Toil and labor cannot weary
Love enduring unto death.
Constant was the love he gave her,
Though he went forth from her side,
Forth to preach and heal and suffer,
Till on Calvary he died.

Glory be to God the Father,
Glory be to God the Son;
Glory be to God the Spirit;
Glory to the Three in One.
From the heart of blessed Mary,
From all saints the song ascends,
And the church the strain re-echoes
Unto earth's remotest ends.

READING (Choose one of the following.)

MOTHER AND SON
JOHN 2:1–5

There was a wedding in Cana of Gal¹   r of
Jesus was there. Jesus and his d·   ed
to the wedding. When the wi   us
said to him, "They have no   to her,
"Woman, what concern is that   ne? My hour
has not yet come." His mot   to the servants,
"Do whatever he tells you."

Paste this page on top of page 78 in the book. We apologize for the inconvenience.

He whom nothing can contain,
No one can compel,
Bound his timeless Godhead here,
In our time to dwell.

God, our Father, Lord of days,
And his only Son,
With the Holy Spirit praise:
Trinity in One.

READING (Choose one of the following.)

OUR LADY OF WISDOM
SIRACH 24:2–7, 19–22

Wisdom opens her mouth,
   and in the presence of his hosts she tells of her glory.
"I came forth from the mouth of the Most High,
   and covered the earth like a mist.
I dwelt in the highest heavens,
   and my throne was in a pillar of cloud.
Alone I compassed the vault of heaven
   and traversed the depths of the abyss.
Over waves of the sea, over all the earth,
   and over every people and nation I have held sway.
Among all these I sought a resting place.

MOTHER OF THE AMERICAS

A NOVENA IN HONOR OF OUR LADY OF GUADALUPE

MOTHER OF THE AMERICAS

A NOVENA IN HONOR OF OUR LADY OF GUADALUPE

WILLIAM G. STOREY

LTP

LITURGY
TRAINING
PUBLICATIONS

ACKNOWLEDGMENTS

We are grateful to the many publishers and authors who have given permission to include their work. Every effort has been made to determine the ownership of all texts and to make proper arrangements for their use. We will gladly correct in future editions any oversight or error that is brought to our attention.

Excerpts from scripture are from the *New Revised Standard Version of the Bible* © 1989, Division of Christian Education of the National Council of the Churches of Christ in the United States of America. Used by permission. All rights reserved.

Acknowledgments continued on p. 89.

MOTHER OF THE AMERICAS: A NOVENA IN HONOR OF OUR LADY OF GUADALUPE © 2003 Archdiocese of Chicago: Liturgy Training Publications, 1800 North Hermitage Avenue, Chicago IL 60622-1101; 1-800-933-1800; fax 1-800-933-7094, e-mail orders@ltp.org. All rights reserved. See our website at www.ltp.org.

This book was edited by Lorie Simmons with assistance from Miguel Arias, Lorraine Schmidt, and Laura Goodman. Kris Fankhouser was the production editor. The design is by Larry Cope, and the typesetting was done by Kari Nicholls in Garamond and Trajan. The cover art is by Julie Lonneman.

Printed in the United States of America.

Library of Congress Control Number: 2003110467

ISBN 1-56854-501-0

MOA

CONTENTS

FOREWORD

Novenas are a very beautiful and powerful tradition in the devotional life of the church. They are easily accessible to anyone and loved by people of all ethnicities and backgrounds. They provide solace, consolation, and hope to the many who pray them with faith.

What could be more beautiful in this day and age than a new novena to Our Lady of Guadalupe, proclaimed by Pope John Paul II as the Mother of America?* She was there at the very birth of the so-called "new world" we know today as America. In what may have been the most painful moment of our hemispheric history, a moment when many of the people had lost all hope and only wanted to die, she came to offer healing and new life to everyone, but especially to those in greatest distress. She came to listen to our laments, to heal our wounds, to defend us as a loving mother, and to welcome all of us into the family home. She reassured us, "You have nothing to fear; am I not here who am your mother?"

Over the ages, she has been there for anyone who calls upon her. Countless miracles are told by the people who have benefited from her intercession. No one needs to promote devotion to her. The testimonies of the healed, the consoled, the protected, and the encouraged continue to increase devotion in her maternal power of intercession. I personally have heard many such testimonies and have no doubt about her living presence among us.

It is a distinct pleasure to introduce you to this beautiful novena in honor of Our Lady of Guadalupe developed by such an eminent scholar and man of faith as William G. Storey, Professor Emeritus of Liturgy of the University of Notre Dame. I have been deeply touched and inspired as I prayed this novena in preparation for this very brief introduction. It joins some of the most beautiful sayings of the fathers of the church with beautiful contemporary thought about Mary. It truly nourishes the mind, the heart, and most of all the spirit. I have no doubt that you will find great comfort and peace in praying this novena, whether alone or together with others. You will experience the presence of Our Lady of Guadalupe, who wants to be with all who come to her and call upon her.

As she did at Cana of Galilee, she will present our needs to her Son who, like any loving son, cannot deny the requests of the mother. She stayed with us, not only on the tilma of Juan Diego, but also in the hearts and minds of all her followers, and she will be with you as you pray this beautiful novena. Thank you, Dr. Storey, for providing us with this wonderful gift, this marvelous novena to Our Lady of Guadalupe, Mother of America.

Virgilio Elizondo

---

*The Holy Father wished to stress the unity of North and South America and so referred to it as one continent.

INTRODUCTION

THE ENCOUNTER BETWEEN JUAN DIEGO
AND MARY, THE MOTHER OF GOD

The most reliable account of the four appearances of Our Lady of Guadalupe was written by a Nahuatl scholar, Don Antonio Valeriano of the Colegio de la Santa Cruz of Tlatelolco, for the Nahuatl people, to whom Juan Diego belonged. From its opening words, it is called the Nican Mopohua, *"Aquí se narra"* or "Here is told." This narrative poem is of great symbolic power and stands as a masterpiece of Nahuatl literature written sometime between 1540 and 1580. Its finest translation into English and fullest theological commentary is by the Reverend Virgilio Elizondo.

The fantastic city of Mexico, the capital of the Aztec Empire, fell to the manipulation and steel of the Spanish conquistadores in 1521. After 10 years the war resulted in a total and humiliating defeat of the Indian population. In the meantime, 12 Franciscan missionaries had arrived and begun the unrelenting suppression of the native religion and the conversion of the conquered nation to Spanish Catholicism. Among the first converts were an Indian named Singing Eagle and his wife. He received the baptismal name of Juan Diego and she the name Maria Lucia (1524 or 1525). They were poor laborers *(campesinos)* and had no children. His wife died in 1529 and Juan Diego moved in with his uncle Juan Bernardino to help him in his old age and in order to be nearer the center of evangelization and liturgy where he could receive religious instruction and attend Mass.

FIRST ENCOUNTER WITH THE VIRGIN

Our story begins on Saturday, December 9, 1531, when Juan Diego was 57 years old and on his way to Mass. He was pursuing his long night walk across the rugged countryside until, around dawn, he reached a small hill called Tepeyac. Suddenly Juan heard a variety of beautiful birdsongs coming from the top of the hill. It amazed him and made him wonder if perhaps he had been caught up into another world. After the birds stopped singing he heard a voice from the summit of the hill: *"Dignified Juan, dignified Juan Diego."* Without fear he mounted the hill until he saw a lady of perfect beauty standing there. She seemed clothed with the sun whose rays illumined the top of the hill until its rocks shone like jewels and its foliage sparkled like gold.

As Juan bowed before her, she spoke: *"Listen, dignified Juan, the least of my sons; where are you going?"* Juan responded that he was going into Tlatelolco for priestly instruction and to attend Mass. Then Mary told him who she was and what she wanted of him, saying: *"Know and be certain in your heart, my most abandoned son, that I am the Ever-Virgin Holy Mary, Mother of the God of Great Truth, Teotl, of the One through Whom We live, the Creator of Persons, the Owner of What is Near and Together, of the Lord of Heaven and Earth. I very much want and ardently desire that my hermitage be erected in this place. In it I will show and give to all people all my love, my compassion, my help, and my protection, because I am your merciful Mother and the mother of all the nations that live on this earth who would love me, who would speak with me, who would search for me, and who would place their confidence in me. There I will hear all their laments and remedy and cure all their miseries, misfortunes, and sorrows"* (Nican Mopohua, #21–25).

She told Juan that he was to be her messenger to the bishop of Mexico to tell him of all that he had heard and seen, and that she wanted the bishop to build her a home, a temple at Tepeyac. She also promised Juan that she would repay him for his trouble by making him joyful and happy if he carried out her command. Without any hesitation Juan Diego replied, "I am already on the way to make your word a reality" (NM, #28).

First Interview with Bishop Juan de Zumárraga

In Mexico City he went directly to the bishop-elect's palace and after a long delay was admitted to his presence. Juan knelt before the bishop and told him all that he had heard and seen at Tepeyac. The bishop listened but was not impressed by either Juan Diego or his request and turned Juan away, saying he would speak of such things at another time.

Second Encounter with the Virgin

A saddened Juan left the bishop's presence and took the road back to Tepeyac where the Lady was waiting for him. He explained his unsatisfactory interview and begged Mary to send someone else of greater dignity who might get an audience to speak on her behalf. Mary replied that he was the only messenger she wanted and that her desires would be accomplished through him alone. In fact, she ordered Juan to go back to the bishop the very next day and repeat her request: *"Tell him once again that I personally, the Ever-Virgin Mary, the Mother of God, Teotl, am the one who is sending you there"* (NM, #24).

THE SECOND INTERVIEW WITH THE BISHOP

The next day, Sunday, December 10, he again went to Mass at Tlatelolco and then into Mexico City to see the bishop. He had an even harder time getting admitted this time. He begged and pleaded with the bishop to listen to the Virgin's pleas but Bishop Zumárraga was not to be persuaded by mere words. He demanded some sign from heaven to authenticate such an unusual request. Impressed by Juan's persistence but not convinced, the bishop dismissed him. This time the Lady from Heaven was not waiting for him at Tepeyac so Juan returned home to find his uncle deathly ill and desiring a priest to prepare him for death.

THIRD ENCOUNTER WITH THE VIRGIN, DECEMBER 12

Early on Tuesday, December 12, Juan Diego hurried to call a priest and decided to skirt Tepeyac for fear he would again encounter Mary and be delayed on his errand of mercy. Mary, however, was waiting there, blocked his passage, and again wanted to know where he was going. Juan carefully explained his dilemma about his dying uncle and promised to carry out her mission the next day.

The Virgin answered, *"Am I not here, your mother? Are you not under my shadow and my protection? Am I not your source of life? Are you not in the hollow of my mantle where I cross my arms? Who else do you need? Let nothing trouble you or cause you sorrow. Do not worry because of your uncle's sickness. He will not die of his present sickness. Be assured in your heart that he is already healed"* (NM, #76–77).

After she quieted his fears, Juan begged her to send him back with the sign the bishop wanted so that this time he would be believed. By way of answer she sent him to the top of the hill where he had first seen her and asked him to pick the exquisite flowers he found blooming there despite the season and the temperature. Carrying them in the hollow of his mantle, he came down and presented them to the Queen of heaven who rearranged them in his mantle and ordered him to carry them to the bishop as the proof, the sign of what she wanted. *"You are my ambassador; in you I place all my trust. . . . With this you will change the heart of the lord of the priests so that he will do his part to build and erect the temple that I have asked him for"* (NM, #87–88). Juan immediately took the road to Mexico City again, "enjoying the scent of the beautiful flowers" (NM, #89).

THIRD INTERVIEW WITH THE BISHOP

At the palace Juan was treated even more rudely than usual. He was forced to wait most of the day until the servants were so intrigued by what he might have hidden in his mantle that they finally announced his presence to Bishop Zumárraga. "Upon hearing this the lord bishop realized this meant that the despicable man had the proof to convince him and bring about what he asked for" (NM, #97).

Juan Diego then rehearsed all that had happened and how the precious Mother of God had complied with the bishop's wishes for a sign. At that he unfolded his white mantle, and the various flowers from Castile fell to the ground. "In that very moment she painted herself: the precious image of the Ever-Virgin, Holy Mary, Mother of God, Teotl appeared suddenly just as she is today and is kept in her precious home, in her hermitage of Tepeyac" (NM, #107).

CONVERSION OF THE BISHOP

The bishop and his attendants fell to their knees in amazement and the bishop begged her to forgive his unbelief. "When he stood up, he untied the mantle from Juan Diego's neck, the mantle in which had appeared and was painted the

Lady from Heaven. Then he took her and went to place her in his oratory" (NM, #110).

THE FIRST CONSTRUCTION OF THE HERMITAGE

The next day, December 13, Juan and the bishop went to see the spot where the Virgin wanted her house built and the bishop invited people to build it. Now that his task was finished Juan decided to return home to see his uncle and some of the bishop's household insisted on going with him.

THE FOURTH APPARITION AND FIRST MIRACLE

When they arrived they found Uncle Juan Bernardino in good health. Juan was obliged to explain the presence of the entourage and briefly related the story of what had happened. In turn, Uncle Bernardino related how he had been healed by the Virgin and that she had appeared exactly to him as she had appeared to his nephew. He also said that the Virgin told him to go into Mexico City and tell the bishop the whole story of his healing.

"They took Juan Bernardino to the bishop so that he might speak and witness before him. And, together with his nephew Juan Diego, he was hosted by the bishop in his home for several days, until the hermitage of the Queen and Lady from Heaven was built at Tepeyac, where Juan Diego had seen her" (NM, #120–121).

MARIAN DEVOTION

Devotion to the Mother of God is a mark of the Catholic Christian. Mary is the Virgin, the Mother, the woman par excellence, and the One who cares for everyone. The earliest surviving prayer to her—in Greek and Coptic and issuing from the Church of Alexandria of the late second or early third century—became a part of both Eastern and Western liturgies:

> We turn to you for protection,
> holy Mother of God (Theotokos).
> Listen to our prayers
> and help us in our needs.
> Save us from every danger,
> glorious and blessed Virgin.

Ever since the Ecumenical Council of Ephesus (431) vindicated this essential title of Theotokos (Mother of God) against those theologians and bishops who denied its perfect propriety and preferred to call her only the Mother of Christ, the Catholic and Orthodox churches have elaborated liturgies and devotions of every sort to exalt Mary as Theotokos. Churches, shrines, poetry, hymnody, sermons, and works of art flourish in her honor. Great Marian pilgrimage centers draw millions of devout pilgrims each year to sing her praise and to implore her assistance in every need.

In the new world of America, Guadalupe is the preeminent pilgrimage center to the holy Mother of God. No other Marian shrine carries such marks of authenticity and popularity as Guadalupe. Under the title of Our Lady of Guadalupe, Mary is the patroness of North and South America and her feast of December 12 lies at the heart of the season of Advent. Her miraculous picture, "not-made-by-human-hands," impressed on the mantle of Saint Juan Diego, is the central feature of the great basilica that contains it.

The "great Mother of God, Mary most holy" has a string of feasts in the liturgy and almost innumerable pilgrimage centers throughout the world. But the great shrine church of Our Lady of Guadalupe on Mount Tepeyac outside of Mexico City is the earliest, the most renowned, and the most inspiring pilgrimage center to the Virgin Mary in the New World. The dark Virgin summons pilgrims from the whole of North and South America to her shrine and to fervent forms of private and communal prayer in her honor. From the beginning she wanted to be known as Mother and special protector of the poor, the downtrodden, and the wretched of the earth:

> *"I will show and give to all people all my love, my compassion, my help, and my protection. I am your merciful mother and the mother of all the nations. . . . I will hear their laments and remedy and cure all their miseries, misfortunes, and sorrows."* (NM, #23–25)

NOVENAS

A novena is nine days of private or public prayer. It probably derives from the nine days of prayer that prepare for the feast of Christmas in Spain and France. Even in our time, *Las Posadas, jornada de María santísima y San José de Nazaret a Belén* (the shelters, the journey of Holy Mary and Saint Joseph from Nazareth to Bethlehem) are widely observed throughout Mexico and the Southwest of the United States from December 16 to December 24.

Novenas are an expression of our faith and trust in the promises of Jesus in the Sermon on the Mount:

> "Ask, and it will be given you; search, and you will find; knock, and the door will be opened for you. For everyone who asks receives, and everyone who searches finds, and for everyone who knocks, the door will be opened. Is there anyone among you who, if your child asks for bread, will give a stone? Or if the child asks for a fish, will give a snake? If you then, you who are

evil, know how to give good gifts to your children, how much more will your Father in heaven give good things to those who ask him? (Matthew 7:7–11)

Novenas also express our belief in the communion of saints and in the preeminent and indispensable role of the Blessed Virgin Mary in that universal communion of holy things and holy people. She is the Mother of Jesus and the Mother of his church and of each baptized person in it. All who are baptized are bonded together in the body of Christ and rest in the hollow of the mantle where Mary crosses her arms.

A Marian novena is a time of special devotion to the Mother of God and can be celebrated on various occasions for a variety of intentions: as a spiritual preparation for one of Mary's many feast days; for a recovery from illness, for a good marriage, for a conversion, for deliverance from temptation, for success in an undertaking, for rescue from danger, for our loved ones who have fallen asleep in Christ, and for the reign of peace and justice in the world.

NOVENA TO OUR LADY OF GUADALUPE

Relying on the wonderful promises of the Lady from Heaven, novenas were observed in her shrine church at Tepeyac from a very early period. This novena offers a way to pray with heightened awareness of Mary's love and protection while reflecting on the events of her life through scripture and other writings from the tradition. This novena may be used, in private and in public, throughout the year:

1) in preparation for one or more of Mary's feasts as they appear in the liturgical calendar;

2) in preparation for her patronal feast day on December 12, the day of her last appearance to Juan Diego at the hill of Tepeyac;

3) as a perpetual novena in honor of Our Lady on the twelfth day of each month;

4) in preparation for the birthday, name day, or baptismal day of anyone bearing the name of Mary (Maria, Miriam, Marian) or of any of her titles, such as Asunción, Concepción, Encarnación, Santa Maria de la Encarnación, Rosario, Nuestra Señora de Guadalupe (Lupe), Dolores, Our Lady of Mount Carmel, Luján, Fátima, Lourdes, Charity, Divine Providence, and so forth;

5) as a novena of prayer for a special need on nine successive days at any time of the year;

6) as a novena of prayer for a special intention on nine Saturdays or on nine first Saturdays of the month;

7) as a form of devotion for every Saturday throughout the year, Saturday being especially dedicated to the Mother of God;

8) as a novena of prayer for the faithful departed, especially during the first nine days after the death of a loved one and as an annual memorial;

9) as a kind of Little Office of Saint Mary, that may be repeated daily in a cycle of nine days.

This novena is meant for individuals and groups. In both cases attention should be centered on a picture of

Our Lady of Guadalupe on the home altar or in a church or chapel, surrounded by candles and flowers.

Whether the faithful pray by themselves or in a group, they are united with all Christian believers in heaven and on earth. No baptized person is ever alone in prayer. We are all united in the indwelling Holy Spirit, brothers and sisters of Jesus, the children of Mary, our Mother, and the daughters and sons of Abba, our dear heavenly Father.

Those who pray this novena with family or other Christians will want to consider certain conditions for peaceful and reverent group prayer:

1) If small children are part of the group, these prayer forms will have to be abbreviated for their sake. The attention span of young children is short; long prayers will bore and alienate them. In this case, "less is more."

2) "Haste is the death of devotion" (Saint Francis de Sales). Each group must set a pace for itself that is respectful of the divine presence and of the needs of the people present, who may vary in age and liturgical experience.

3) In these services of prayer, parts are meant to be alternated between a leader and the group, with additional help from a reader for the lessons from scripture. The stanzas of the hymns and canticles are recited in turn by the leader and the group. There is an interpretative antiphon before each canticle. The leader begins the antiphon and all recite it in unison both before and after the canticle.

4) Two pauses are suggested—one after the reading (for meditation) and another at the end of the litany (for spontaneous prayers of intercession). These are

important parts of the novena; the leader will decide how long they should be.

5) Groups may alternate standing, sitting, and kneeling. Stand from the beginning to the reading; sit for the reading and meditation; stand for the canticle; kneel for the closing prayers. A cross (+) appears in the text when it is appropriate to make the sign of the cross.

6) The Our Father, Hail Mary, and Glory to the Father may be added.

7) A kiss of peace may be exchanged by all at the end of the novena service.

THE FIRST DAY: MARY'S BIRTHDAY

Mary's birthday is the inauguration of the era of grace for all of humanity. Just as Eve, the mother of us all, came fresh from the creative hand of God, so Mary comes into the world immaculate, grace-filled, and the mother of us all in the order of grace. Saint John of Damascus set forth the theme of this celebration in the seventh century: "Let everyone come to this feast; with joy let us celebrate the beginning of joy for the whole world! Today heaven begins on earth; today is the inauguration of salvation for the whole world." Let us wish our Blessed Mother a happy birthday because by so doing we discover a new reason for rejoicing in the universality of her loving motherhood and her constant intercession for us.

ON THE BIRTHDAY OF THE BLESSED VIRGIN MARY

The much desired feast of Blessed Mary ever Virgin has come; so let our land, illumined by such a birth, be glad with great rejoicing. For she is the flower of the field from whom bloomed the precious Lily of the valley, through whose birth that nature inherited from our first parents is changed and guilt is blotted out. Eve mourned, Mary rejoiced. Eve carried tears in her heart; Mary, joy. For Eve gave birth to men of sin, Mary to the Innocent One. The mother of our race brought punishment upon the world, the Mother of our Lord brought salvation into the world. Eve was the author of sin, Mary the authoress of merit; Eve by killing was a hindrance, Mary by giving life was a help; Eve struck, and Mary healed. Disobedience is displaced by obedience, and fidelity atones for infidelity.

Now let Mary play upon musical instruments and let timbrels reverberate under the fleet fingers of this young Mother. Let joyous choirs sing together harmoniously, and let sweet songs be blended now with one melody and now with another. Hear how our timbrel player has sung. For she said, "My soul magnifies the Lord and my spirit rejoices in God my Savior, because He has regarded the lowliness of His handmaid; for behold, henceforth all generations shall call me blessed; because He who is mighty has done great things for me." This miraculous new birth has utterly vanquished the root of aimless wanderings; Mary's canticle has ended the lamentations of Eve.

—Saint Augustine, Bishop of Hippo, 354–430

CALL TO PRAYER

Leader: Blessed be the great Mother of God,
         Mary most holy!

All: *~Whose splendid nativity enlightens
         all the churches.*

Leader: Hail, Mary, full of grace, the Lord is with you.

All: *~Blessed are you among women.*

HYMN

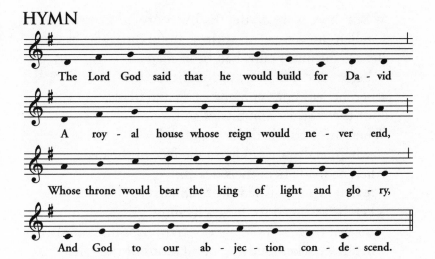

The Lord God said that he would build for Da-vid

A roy-al house whose reign would ne-ver end,

Whose throne would bear the king of light and glo-ry,

And God to our ab-jec-tion con-de-scend.

From Jesse's root came forth the Virgin Mary,
Who bore the world's redeemer, Christ our Lord,
The Son of God, by his most Holy Spirit:
His uncreated and eternal Word.

Great mystery no thought could ever fathom,
The saving plan, long fashioned in God's mind,
When Father, Son and Spirit, undivided,
Restore immortal life to mortal kind.

READING (Choose one of the following.)

HOLY WISDOM
PROVERBS 8:22–36

"The LORD created me at the beginning of his work,
    the first of his acts of long ago.
Ages ago I was set up,
    at the first, before the beginning of the earth.

When there were no depths I was brought forth,
    when there were no springs abounding with water.
Before the mountains had been shaped,
    before the hills, I was brought forth—
when he had not yet made earth and fields,
    or the world's first bits of soil.
When he established the heavens, I was there,
    when he drew a circle on the face of the deep,
when he made firm the skies above,
    when he established the fountains of the deep,
when he assigned to the sea its limit,
    so that the waters might not transgress his command,
when he marked out the foundations of the earth,
    then I was beside him, like a master worker;
and I was daily his delight,
rejoicing before him always,
rejoicing in his inhabited world
and delighting in the human race.
And now, my children, listen to me:
    happy are those who keep my ways.
Hear instruction and be wise,
    and do not neglect it.
Happy is the one who listens to me,
    watching daily at my gates,
    waiting beside my doors.
For whoever finds me finds life
    and obtains favor from the LORD;
but those who miss me injure themselves;
    all who hate me love death."

SILENCE

RESPONSE

Leader: Today is the birthday of the Virgin Mother,
alleluia!

All: ~*Whose life illuminates the whole church, alleluia!*

(Or this)

SACRED GENEALOGY
MATTHEW 1:1–2, 5C–6, 16

An account of the genealogy of Jesus the Messiah, the son of David, the son of Abraham. Abraham was the father of Isaac, and Isaac the father of Jacob, and Jacob the father of Judah and his brothers, and Obed the father of Jesse, and Jesse the father of King David. And David was the father of Solomon by the wife of Uriah, and Jacob the father of Joseph the husband of Mary, of whom Jesus was born, who is called the Messiah.

SILENCE

RESPONSE

Leader: Great is the faith of Mary the Virgin!

All: ~*All that God promised her will come true.*

CANTICLE OF THE BLESSED VIRGIN MARY
LUKE 1:46–55

Leader: Great Mother of God,

All: *~Your birth brings joy to the whole universe,*
          for from you arose the Sun of righteousness,
          Christ our Lord,
          who abolished death
          and gives us life eternal, alleluia!

My soul pro - claims the great - ness of the Lord,

My spir - it sings to God, my sav - ing God,

Who on this day a - bove all oth - ers fa - vored me

And raised me up, a light for all to see.

Through me great deeds will God make manifest,
And all the earth will come to call me blest.
Unbounded love and mercy sure will I proclaim
For all who know and praise God's holy name.

God's mighty arm, protector of the just,
Will guard the weak and raise them from the dust.
But mighty kings will swiftly fall from thrones corrupt.
The strong brought low, the lowly lifted up.

Soon will the poor and hungry of the earth
Be richly blest, be given greater worth.
And Israel, as once foretold to Abraham,
Will live in peace throughout the promised land.

All glory be to God, Creator blest,
To Jesus Christ, God's love made manifest,
And to the Holy Spirit, gentle Comforter,
All glory be, both now and evermore. Amen.

All: *~Great Mother of God,*
your birth brings joy to the whole universe,
for from you arose the Sun of righteousness,
Christ our Lord, who abolished death
and gives us life eternal, alleluia!

LITANY (see pages 84–88)

PRAYER

Leader: Let us pray:
Father of mercy,
give your people help and strength from heaven.
The birth of the Virgin Mary's Son
was the dawn of our salvation.
May this celebration of her birthday
bring us closer to lasting peace.
We ask this through Christ our Lord.

All: *~Amen.*

NOVENA PRAYER

Leader: Holy Mother of God and Queen of Heaven,

All: *~At Tepeyac you promised to show*
all the nations of the earth
your love, compassion, help, and protection.
Because you are our merciful mother,
hear our laments, and remedy all our miseries,
*   misfortunes, and sorrows.*
Stamp your priceless image on our hearts,
unveil your precious will for us,
and hold us in the hollow of your mantle
where you cross your arms,
now and always and for ever and ever.
Amen.

BLESSING

Leader: May the Virgin Mary mild
+ bless us with her holy Child.

All: *~Amen.*

THE SECOND DAY:
GOOD NEWS FOR MARY

So early in the history of the church that we cannot document it, March 25 was considered the day that both opened and closed Jesus' life, that is, the day on which he was conceived in the womb of the Virgin Mary at the message of an angel and also the day on which he died on the cross for us on the hill of Golgotha. One of the oldest prayers in the Roman tradition refers to this most ancient view of March 25 and is used here. It is also the prayer used for the Angelus three times a day.

Mary's "Yes" to the angelic message made her the highly favored daughter of God the Father, the mother of God the Son, and our model of willing and complete obedience to the call of the Holy Spirit in our lives.

THEOTOKOS

He who was divinely generated by the Father before all ages, the Same is generated by a Virgin today, for our salvation's sake. There above, he is the only Son, generated according to divinity, by the only Father; here below he is God, but not just a man according to humanity. There above, he is with the Father in an inexpressible way; here below, he is born from his Mother in an unspeakable way. There above, he has no mother; here below, he has no earthly father. Above, the Firstborn, before all ages; below, the firstborn of a Virgin, according to the mystery of the incarnation. Precisely for this reason, the Virgin is Mother of God. Thus, even after giving birth, she remained a virgin.

The birth is inexplicable because of the inaccessible mystery, but the Word became visible through the event of his incarnation. Consider that he remained what he was and became what he was not, passible and impassible together, according to what was seen, remaining consubstantial with the Father according to his divinity and consubstantial with us according to his humanity, except in the matter of sin.

—*Saint Proclus, Patriarch of Constantinople, 434–446*

CALL TO PRAYER

Leader: Blessed be the great Mother of God,
Mary most holy!

All: *~She conceived Emmanuel in her womb!*

Leader: Mary is more worthy of honor than the cherubim

All: *~And far more glorious than the seraphim.*

HYMN

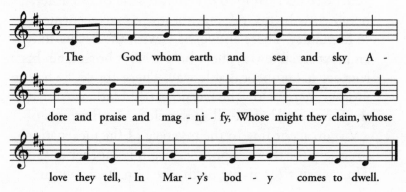

The God whom earth and sea and sky Adore and praise and mag-ni-fy, Whose might they claim, whose love they tell, In Mar-y's bod-y comes to dwell.

O Mother blest! The chosen shrine
Wherein the architect divine
Whose hand contains the earth and sky,
Has come in human form to lie:

Blest in the message Gabriel brought;
Blest in the work the Spirit wrought;
Most blest, to bring to human birth
The long desired of all the earth.

O Lord, the Virgin born, to you
Eternal praise and laud are due,
Whom with the Father we adore
And Spirit blest for evermore.

READING (Choose one of the following.)

MARY'S FREE CONSENT
LUKE 1:35, 37–38

The angel said to Mary: "The Holy Spirit will come upon you, and the power of the Most High will overshadow you; therefore the child to be born will be holy; he will be called Son of God. For nothing will be impossible with God." Then Mary said: "Here am I, the servant of the Lord; let it be with me according to your word." Then the angel departed from her.

SILENCE

RESPONSE

Leader: The Word was made flesh, alleluia!

All: ~*And came to live among us, alleluia!*

(Or this)

Eternal Life
1 John 1:1–3

We declare to you what was from the beginning, what we have heard, what we have seen with our eyes, what we have looked at and touched with our hands, concerning the word of life—this life was revealed, and we have seen it and testify to it, and declare to you the eternal life that was with the Father and was revealed to us—we declare to you what we have seen and heard so that you also may have fellowship with us; and truly our fellowship is with the Father and with his Son Jesus Christ.

SILENCE

RESPONSE

Leader: The Holy Spirit will come upon you, Mary, alleluia!

All: ~*And the power of the Most High will overshadow you, alleluia!*

CANTICLE OF THE BLESSED VIRGIN MARY
LUKE 1:46–55

Leader: Today is the beginning of our salvation

All: ~*And the revelation of the eternal mystery:
         the Son of God becomes the Son of the Virgin Mary
         as Gabriel announces the good news of God's grace.*

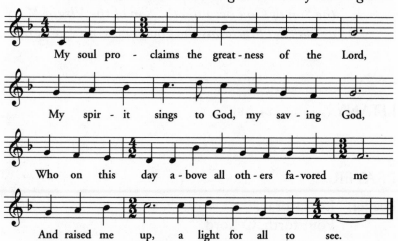

My soul pro - claims the great-ness of the Lord,

My spir - it sings to God, my sav - ing God,

Who on this day a - bove all oth-ers fa-vored me

And raised me up, a light for all to see.

Through me great deeds will God make manifest,
And all the earth will come to call me blest.
Unbounded love and mercy sure will I proclaim
For all who know and praise God's holy name.

God's mighty arm, protector of the just,
Will guard the weak and raise them from the dust.
But mighty kings will swiftly fall from thrones corrupt.
The strong brought low, the lowly lifted up.

Soon will the poor and hungry of the earth
Be richly blest, be given greater worth.
And Israel, as once foretold to Abraham,
Will live in peace throughout the promised land.

All glory be to God, Creator blest,
To Jesus Christ, God's love made manifest,
And to the Holy Spirit, gentle Comforter,
All glory be, both now and evermore. Amen.

All: *~Today is the beginning of our salvation*
and the revelation of the eternal mystery:
the Son of God becomes the Son of the Virgin Mary
as Gabriel proclaims the good news of God's grace.

LITANY (see pages 84–88)

PRAYER

Leader: Let us pray:
Pour forth, O Lord,
your grace into our hearts,
that we to whom the incarnation of Christ your Son
was made known by the message of an angel,
may by his passion and death
be brought to the glory of his resurrection.
Through the same Christ our Lord.

All: *~Amen.*

NOVENA PRAYER

Leader: Holy Mother of God and Queen of Heaven,

All: *~At Tepeyac you promised to show*
all the nations of the earth
your love, compassion, help, and protection.
Because you are our merciful mother,
hear our laments, and remedy all our miseries,
     misfortunes, and sorrows.
Stamp your priceless image on our hearts,
unveil your precious will for us,
and hold us in the hollow of your mantle
where you cross your arms,
now and always and for ever and ever.
Amen.

BLESSING

Leader: May the Virgin Mary mild
+ bless us with her holy Child.

All: *~Amen.*

THE THIRD DAY:
THE BIRTHDAY OF JESUS

In the gospels Jesus on the lap of Mary is the center of the Christmas story. There in the sacred cave cut in the hillside she brought forth the Son of God and then presented him to awestruck shepherds and adoring wise men from the East. That is how Christians see her, especially at Christmas, and that is how she is often portrayed in the sacred art of every century, in countless paintings, sculptures and icons in cathedrals and parish churches, in homes and outdoor shrines. The child Jesus, in the arms or on the lap of Mary, and the crucified Jesus, with Mary standing at the foot of the cross, are the central pictures that adorn our homes and churches because they express the central themes of the gospel: God incarnate in human form and the same Jesus suffering and dying for our salvation with Mary at his side.

THE INCARNATION

The Word was made flesh and dwells now among us. He dwells in our memory, He dwells in our reflections, for he goes down even into our imagination. You ask in what way. Why, truly, lying in the manger, cradled in the womb, preaching on the mountain, praying through the night, hanging on the cross, growing pale in death, free among the dead and giving his commands in hell, rising the third day, and showing to the apostles the marks of his victory, imparting to them in a new way the secrets of heaven. From which of these things does not reflection draw truth, holiness, and worship?

When I meditate on these things I meditate on God
and through them all he is my God.
— *Saint Bernard of Clairvaux, 1090–1153*

CALL TO PRAYER

Leader: Blessed be the great Mother of God,
Mary most holy!

All: *~She bore the Son of the eternal Father!*

Leader: Glory to God in the highest, alleluia!

All: *~And peace to God's people on earth, alleluia!*

HYMN

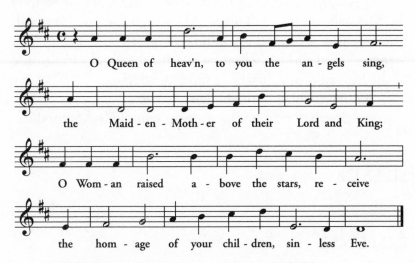

O Queen of heav'n, to you the an - gels sing,

the Maid - en - Moth - er of their Lord and King;

O Wom - an raised a - bove the stars, re - ceive

the hom - age of your chil - dren, sin - less Eve.

O full of grace, in grace your womb did bear
Emmanuel, King David's promised heir;

Text: *Salve Regina*, tr. James Quinn, SJ. Text © James Quinn, SJ. Selah Publishing Co., Inc., North American agent,
www.selahpub.com

O Eastern Gate, whom God had made his own,
By you God's glory came to Zion's throne.

O Burning Bush, you gave the world its light
When Christ your Son was born on Christmas night;
O Mary Queen, who bore God's holy One,
For us, your children, pray to God your Son. Amen.

READING (Choose one of the following.)

THE NATIVITY OF JESUS
LUKE 2:10–14

The angel said to the shepherds, "Do not be afraid; for see—
I am bringing you good news of great joy for all the people:
to you is born this day in the city of David a Savior, who is
the Messiah, the Lord. This will be a sign for you: you will
find a child wrapped in bands of cloth and lying in a
manger." And suddenly there was with the angel a multitude
of the heavenly host, praising God and saying,
    "Glory to God in the highest heaven,
    and on earth peace among those whom God favors!"

SILENCE

RESPONSE

Leader: The Word was made flesh, alleluia!

All: *~And came to live among us, alleluia!*

(Or this)

THE MAGI AND THEIR GIFTS
Matthew 2:9–11

> When the Magi had heard the king, they set out; and there ahead of them, went the star that they had seen at its rising, until it stopped over the place where the child was. When they saw that the star had stopped, they were overwhelmed with joy. On entering the house, they saw the child with Mary his mother; and they knelt down and paid him homage. Then, opening their treasure chests, they offered him gifts of gold, frankincense, and myrrh.

SILENCE

RESPONSE

Leader: All the ends of the earth have seen, alleluia!

All: *~The salvation of our God, alleluia!*

CANTICLE OF THE BLESSED VIRGIN MARY
LUKE 1:46–55

Leader: The Child to be born of you, O Mary,

All: *~Will be called the Son of God, alleluia!*

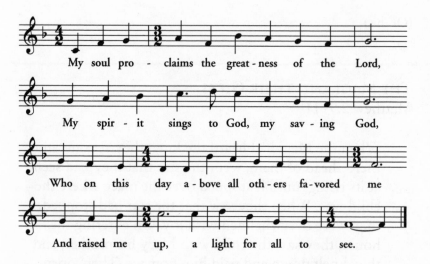

My soul proclaims the greatness of the Lord,
My spirit sings to God, my saving God,
Who on this day above all others favored me
And raised me up, a light for all to see.

Through me great deeds will God make manifest,
And all the earth will come to call me blest.
Unbounded love and mercy sure will I proclaim
For all who know and praise God's holy name.

God's mighty arm, protector of the just,
Will guard the weak and raise them from the dust.
But mighty kings will swiftly fall from thrones corrupt.
The strong brought low, the lowly lifted up.

Soon will the poor and hungry of the earth
Be richly blest, be given greater worth.
And Israel, as once foretold to Abraham,
Will live in peace throughout the promised land.

All glory be to God, Creator blest,
To Jesus Christ, God's love made manifest,
And to the Holy Spirit, gentle Comforter,
All glory be, both now and evermore. Amen.

All: *~The Child to be born of you, O Mary,*
        will be called the Son of God, alleluia!

LITANY (see pages 84–88)

PRAYER

Leader: Let us pray:
         Father, source of light in every age,
         the virgin conceived and bore your Son
         who is called Wonderful God, Prince of Peace.
         May her prayer, gift of a mother's love,
         be your people's joy through all ages.
         May her response, born of a humble heart,
         draw your Spirit to rest on your people.
         Grant this through Christ our Lord.

All: *~Amen.*

NOVENA PRAYER

Leader: Holy Mother of God and Queen of Heaven,

All: *~At Tepeyac you promised to show*
        all the nations of the earth
        your love, compassion, help, and protection.
        Because you are our merciful mother,
        hear our laments, and remedy all our miseries,
        *   misfortunes, and sorrows.*

Stamp your priceless image on our hearts,
unveil your precious will for us,
and hold us in the hollow of your mantle
where you cross your arms,
now and always and for ever and ever.
Amen.

BLESSING

Leader: May the Word made flesh, full of grace and truth,
+ bless us and keep us.

All: *~Amen.*

The Fourth Day:
The Flight into Egypt and the Slaughter of the Innocents

In the gospel story sorrow soon follows upon joy. No sooner have the shepherds and wise men from the East recognized and proclaimed the newborn Jesus than King Herod the Great, representing the godless and inhumane powers of this world, seeks the child Jesus to destroy him. At the urging of a divine messenger, Jesus, Mary, and Joseph become refugees in a foreign country and stay there for several years until they have God's permission to return from Egypt and settle in Nazareth. In the meantime, Herod, fearing that Jesus might be about to replace his dynasty, orders the slaughter of all young boys in and around Bethlehem. For the shepherds and the Magi, Jesus' coming was joy and exultation; for the mothers of Bethlehem it was inconsolable grief for the death of their newborn babes, and a foreshadowing of the cross that was to come.

In our time, when so many uncounted thousands—even millions—of helpless people flee before the face of military tyrants or economic misery and exploitation, we can identify with the holy family in flight, the innocents weltering in their own blood, and the tears of their lamenting mothers.

THE COMPASSION OF MARY

I saw part of the compassion of our Lady, Saint Mary, for Christ and she were so united in love that the greatness of her love was the cause of the greatness of her pain. For her pain surpassed that of all others, as much as she loved him more than all others. And so all his disciples and all his true lovers suffered greater pains than they did at the death of their own bodies. For I am sure, by my own experience, that the least of them loved him more than they loved themselves. And here I saw a great unity between Christ and us; for when he was in pain we were in pain, and all creatures able to suffer pain suffered with him. And for those who did not know him, their pain was that of all creation, sun and moon, ceased to serve men, and so they were all abandoned in sorrow at that time. So those who loved him suffered pain for their love, and those who did not love him suffered pain because the comfort of all creation failed them.

—*Julian of Norwich, ca. 1342–1423*

CALL TO PRAYER

Leader: Great Mother of God, Mary most holy,

All: *~Stand by us in our afflictions.*

Leader: Blessed are they who mourn,

All: *~For they shall be comforted.*

HYMN

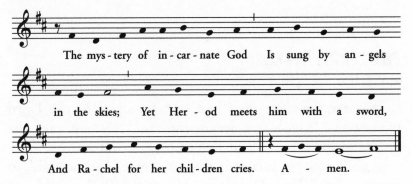

The mys - tery of in - car - nate God Is sung by an - gels in the skies; Yet Her - od meets him with a sword, And Ra - chel for her chil - dren cries. A - men.

Then stained with sorrow is our joy
That Christ is born in flesh on earth;
For shadows of his passion fall
Across the brightness of his birth.

Yet, Jesus, we now give you thanks,
Because the promise has been given
That tears shall all be wiped away,
And love and mercy reign in heaven.

And in your new Jerusalem
Shall hate and love be reconciled;
And wildest wolf and lion and bear
Be led transfigured by a child.

All praise to you, O virgin-born,
Made flesh in our humanity,
To Father and to Paraclete,
Both now and in eternity.

READING (Choose one of the following.)

THE FLIGHT TO EGYPT
MATTHEW 2:13–15

Now after the wise men had left, an angel of the Lord appeared to Joseph in a dream and said, "Get up, take the child and his mother, and flee to Egypt, and remain there until I tell you; for Herod is about to search for the child, to destroy him." Then Joseph got up, and took the child and his mother by night, and went to Egypt, and remained there until the death of Herod.

SILENCE

RESPONSE

Leader: Precious in the sight of the LORD

All: ~Is the death of the saints.

(Or this)

THE HOLY INNOCENTS
MATTHEW 2:16–18

When Herod saw that he had been tricked by the wise men, he was infuriated, and he sent and killed all the [male] children in and around Bethlehem who were two years old or

under, according to the time that he had learned from the wise men. Then was fulfilled what had been spoken through the prophet Jeremiah:
"A voice was heard in Ramah,
wailing and loud lamentation,
Rachel weeping for her children;
she refused to be consoled, because they are no more."

SILENCE

RESPONSE

Leader: Let the holy innocents rejoice in their glory

All: *~Shout for joy and take their rest.*

CANTICLE OF THE BLESSED VIRGIN MARY
LUKE 1:46–55

Leader: A voice was heard in Ramah,

All: *~Wailing and loud lamentation, Rachel weeping for her children.*

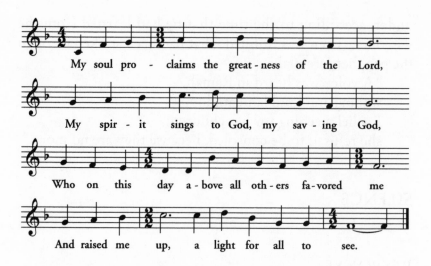

My soul pro - claims the great-ness of the Lord,

My spir - it sings to God, my sav - ing God,

Who on this day a - bove all oth - ers fa - vored me

And raised me up, a light for all to see.

Through me great deeds will God make manifest,
And all the earth will come to call me blest.
Unbounded love and mercy sure will I proclaim
For all who know and praise God's holy name.

God's mighty arm, protector of the just,
Will guard the weak and raise them from the dust.
But mighty kings will swiftly fall from thrones corrupt.
The strong brought low, the lowly lifted up.

Soon will the poor and hungry of the earth
Be richly blest, be given greater worth.
And Israel, as once foretold to Abraham,
Will live in peace throughout the promised land.

All glory be to God, Creator blest,
To Jesus Christ, God's love made manifest,
And to the Holy Spirit, gentle Comforter,
All glory be, both now and evermore. Amen.

All: *~A voice was heard in Ramah,*
Wailing and loud lamentation, Rachel weeping
for her children.

LITANY (see pages 84–88)

PRAYER

Leader: Let us pray:
Lord Jesus, from the beginning
the mighty have resisted your reign
 of justice, peace, and love.
Pity the refugees, the homeless,
 and the persecuted
who flee before the Herods of this world.
Pull down the tyrants from their thrones
and lift up the lowly;
fill the hungry with good things
and send the rich away empty.
For you are the righteousness of God,
who lives and reigns, now and for ever.

All: *~Amen.*

NOVENA PRAYER

Leader: Holy Mother of God and Queen of Heaven,

All: *~At Tepeyac you promised to show*
all the nations of the earth
your love, compassion, help, and protection.

Because you are our merciful mother,
hear our laments, and remedy all our miseries,
*   misfortunes, and sorrows.*
Stamp your priceless image on our hearts,
unveil your precious will for us,
and hold us in the hollow of your mantle
where you cross your arms,
now and always and for ever and ever.
Amen.

BLESSING

Leader: Through the Virgin Mother's prayers,
         may the Lord + grant us safety and peace.

All: *~Amen.*

THE FIFTH DAY: CANA OF GALILEE

In John's gospel we see Jesus and Mary together only twice: once at Cana and once at the Cross. The first time was at the wedding feast of Cana, a tiny village northwest of Nazareth, the home town of Nathanael whom Jesus had called to be his disciple just a day earlier. On the occasion of this small festive gathering, Jesus and his newly chosen disciples and his mother were present at the wedding banquet. When the wine gave out, Mary noticed this embarrassing fact and drew Jesus' attention to it. She must have realized his power to intervene effectively and was not put off by his "My hour has not yet come." Instead, she turned to the servers and said simply, "Do whatever he tells you." The immediate result was the water-made-wine sign of the beginning of the messianic kingdom. "Jesus did this, the first of his signs, in Cana of Galilee, and revealed his glory; and his disciples believed in him" (John 2:11). Mary expected Jesus to be able to do wonders; that is, she already believed in him and in his mission! When next we see her, standing at the foot of the Cross, she is present for the consummation of his life's mission (John 19:25–27). Mary came to believe in the mission of her Son before the rest of his family did. Some of them, at least, thought he was out of his mind and tried to restrain him from further angering the religious and political authorities and endangering his life—and perhaps theirs (Mark 3:21). Jesus took this opportunity to tell us that faith and obedience to the will of God are of greater consequence than blood relationship (Mark 3:31–35). As Jesus went his way in obedience to his Father, Mary had to watch him go his singular path while she prayed and waited for the inevitable outcome.

WATER MADE WINE

Christ's first miracle was performed at the celebration of an earthly union, at a wedding so joyous that the wine failed, and he had to change water into wine in six stone jars intended for the ablutions.

Already he had begun his habit of crossing every threshold, of sitting at every table; because it was for sinners he came, for those who were lost. The scandal began at Cana, and lasted until Bethany, up to the time of the last anointing. The man who called himself the Son of God went every day among publicans, courtesans, the dissolute, the derelict. At Cana there were those who lived riotously and could not forego jests and laughter. The steward of the feast said to the bridegroom: "Every man sets forth good wine at first, and after they have drunk freely then that which is poorer; but you have kept the good wine until now" (John 2:10). It is impossible to doubt that the contents of the six jars added to the joy of a wedding party already well filled with wine. More than one abstemious person put to Christ the hypocritical question which came up so often in the talk of the Pharisees: "Why do the disciples of John fast . . . while your disciples do not fast?" (Mark 2:18). But he smiled and was silent because his hour had not come.

—*François Mauriac, 1885–1970*

CALL TO PRAYER

Leader: Blessed be the great Mother of God,
Mary most holy!

All: *~She commands us to do whatever Jesus tells us.*

Leader: Jesus did this, the first of his signs,
in Cana of Galilee,

All: *~And his disciples believed in him.*

HYMN

Sing of Mar - y, pure and low - ly,
Vir - gin - moth - er un - de - filed.
Sing of God's own Son most ho - ly,
Who be - came her lit - tle child.
Fair - est child of fair - est moth - er,
God the Lord who came to earth
Word made flesh, our ver - y broth - er,
Takes our na - ture by his birth.

Fairest child of fairest mother,
God the Lord who came to earth,
Word made flesh, our very brother,
Takes our nature by his birth.

Sing of Jesus, son of Mary,
In the home of Nazareth.
Toil and labor cannot weary
Love enduring unto death.

Constant was the love he gave her,
Though he went forth from her side,
Forth to preach and heal and suffer,
Till on Calvary he died.

Glory be to God the Father,
Glory be to God the Son;
Glory be to God the Spirit;
Glory to the Three in One.

READING (Choose one of the following.)

MOTHER AND SON
JOHN 2:1–5

There was a wedding in Cana of Galilee, and the mother of Jesus was there. Jesus and his disciples had also been invited to the wedding. When the wine gave out, the mother of Jesus said to him, "They have no wine." And Jesus said to her, "Woman, what concern is that to you and to me? My hour has not yet come." His mother said to the servants, "Do whatever he tells you."

SILENCE

RESPONSE

Leader: Jesus did this and revealed his glory;

All: *~And his disciples believed in him.*

(Or this)

LADY WISDOM SPEAKS
PROVERBS 8:17–21

"I love those who love me,
and those who seek me diligently find me.
Riches and honor are with me,
enduring wealth and prosperity.
My fruit is better than gold, even fine gold,
and my yield than choice silver.
I walk in the way of righteousness,
along the paths of justice,
endowing with wealth those who love me,
and filling their treasuries."

SILENCE

RESPONSE

Leader: The fear of the LORD is the beginning of wisdom.

All: ~*And the knowledge of the Holy One is insight.*

CANTICLE OF THE BLESSED VIRGIN MARY
LUKE 1:46–55

Leader: You shall be a crown of beauty, O Virgin Mary,

All: ~*A royal diadem in the hand of your God, alleluia!*

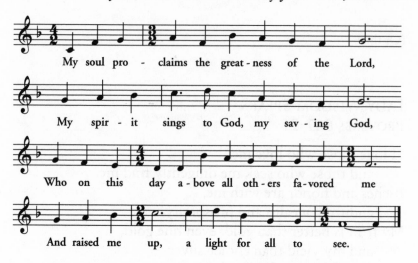

My soul pro - claims the great-ness of the Lord,

My spir - it sings to God, my sav - ing God,

Who on this day a - bove all oth - ers fa - vored me

And raised me up, a light for all to see.

Through me great deeds will God make manifest,
And all the earth will come to call me blest.
Unbounded love and mercy sure will I proclaim
For all who know and praise God's holy name.

God's mighty arm, protector of the just,
Will guard the weak and raise them from the dust.
But mighty kings will swiftly fall from thrones corrupt.
The strong brought low, the lowly lifted up.

Soon will the poor and hungry of the earth
Be richly blest, be given greater worth.
And Israel, as once foretold to Abraham,
Will live in peace throughout the promised land.

All glory be to God, Creator blest,
To Jesus Christ, God's love made manifest,
And to the Holy Spirit, gentle Comforter,
All glory be, both now and evermore. Amen.

All: *~You shall be a crown of beauty, O Virgin Mary,*
         a royal diadem in the hand of your God, alleluia!

LITANY (see pages 84–88)

PRAYER

Leader: Let us pray:
         Abba, dear Father,
         by the overshadowing of the Holy Spirit,
         Mary became the humble and courageous mother
         of the Messiah and Lord of Israel.
         By her unswerving affection toward us,
         may we cling to Jesus, our only teacher,
         and obey him always in thought, word, and deed.
         We ask this through the same Christ our Lord.

All: *~Amen.*

NOVENA PRAYER

Leader: Holy Mother of God and Queen of Heaven,

All: *~At Tepeyac you promised to show*
all the nations of the earth
your love, compassion, help, and protection.
Because you are our merciful mother,
hear our laments, and remedy all our miseries,
*   misfortunes, and sorrows.*
Stamp your priceless image on our hearts,
unveil your precious will for us,
and hold us in the hollow of your mantle
where you cross your arms,
now and always and for ever and ever.
Amen.

BLESSING

Leader: Through the Virgin Mary blest
may the Lord + give us our rest.

All: *~Amen.*

THE SIXTH DAY:
MARY AT THE CROSS

In John's gospel Mary stands at the foot of the cross during the long hours of the crucifixion and Mary holds her dead Son in her arms when he is taken down from the Cross. These scenes are the exact counterpart of Jesus and Mary at the marriage feast of Cana (John 2:1–12). She was there at the beginning of Jesus' public life and occasioned his first sign of extravagant abundance and overflowing generosity. She is there at the end as he dies in agony, surrenders his life to the Father, and leaves her to the care of the disciple whom Jesus loved (John 19:25–30). She is considered a martyr in spirit because she bore witness to her dying Son on the hill of Golgotha and suffered with him until he died and his heart was pierced by a Roman soldier. The hearts of Jesus and Mary are solidly fixed on God and beat in perfect unison as his blessed life draws to a close. She was the first witness of the blood and water that flowed from his heart and became sacraments that give life to the Christian community. Whenever we are present at a baptism or at the eucharistic banquet, we sense her presence as she enjoys the fruits of redemption being extended in time and space down through the ages. She is the mother of the church and of every Christian person.

CHRIST'S LAST WILL AND TESTAMENT

Mary, the mother of the Lord, stood by the cross of her Son. Only Saint John the Evangelist teaches us this. The other evangelists wrote that during the passion of the Lord the world shook, the sky was shrouded in darkness, the sun disappeared, the criminal was admitted into paradise after a devout confession. John taught what the other gospel writers did not teach: how hanging on the cross, Jesus called out to his mother. Now that Jesus, in the midst of his sufferings, thought of his mother is considered more important than his gift of paradise to the repentant felon. If the forgiveness of the criminal was a virtuous act, it was an even greater sign of devotion that the Son should honor his mother with such affection. "Here," he says to Mary, "Here is your son;" to the disciple, "Here is your mother." From the cross Christ made this last will and testament and was dutiful to both his mother and his beloved disciple. The Lord made a will that was both public and private and this will was signed by the disciple whom he loved, a witness worthy of such a testator. It was a fine will, leaving not money but life eternal; written not in ink but by the Spirit of the living God.

—*Saint Ambrose, Bishop of Milan, ca. 339–397*

CALL TO PRAYER

Leader: Blessed be the great Mother of God,
         Mary most holy!

All: *~She stood near Jesus at the foot of the Cross.*

Leader: Blessed is the Virgin Mary, even in her sufferings.

All: *~They won for her the palm of martyrdom.*

HYMN

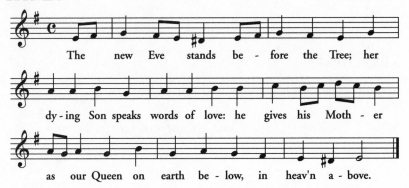

The new Eve stands be - fore the Tree; her
dy - ing Son speaks words of love: he gives his Moth - er
as our Queen on earth be - low, in heav'n a - bove.

The second Adam sleeps in death,
His side is pierced, his heart unsealed;
The grace-filled church, his sinless Bride,
In blood and water is revealed.

We thank you, Father, for the church,
Where Christ is King and Mary Queen,
Where through your Spirit you unfold
A world of glory yet unseen.

READING (Choose one of the following.)

THE SWORD OF SORROW
LUKE 2:34–35

Simeon blessed the parents of Jesus and said to his mother
Mary, "This child is destined for the falling and the rising of
many in Israel, and to be a sign that will be opposed so that
the inner thoughts of many will be revealed—and a sword
will pierce your own soul too."

Text: James Quinn, sj. Text © James Quinn, sj. Selah Publishing Co., Inc., North American agent. www.selahpub.com

SILENCE

RESPONSE

Leader: Through you, O Mother of Sorrows,

All: *~May we draw salvation from Christ's wounds.*

(Or this)

At the Foot of the Cross
JOHN 19:25–27

Standing near the cross of Jesus were his mother, and his mother's sister, Mary the wife of Clopas, and Mary Magdalene. When Jesus saw his mother and the disciple whom he loved standing beside her, he said to his mother, "Woman, here is your son." Then he said to the disciple, "Here is your mother." And from that hour the disciple took her into his own home.

SILENCE

RESPONSE

Leader: The soldier's lance opened our Savior's side,

All: *~And pierced the heart of his sorrowful Mother.*

CANTICLE OF THE BLESSED VIRGIN MARY
LUKE 1:46–55

Leader: Come, let us ascend the mountain of the Lord,

All: ~*And see if there is any sorrow like my sorrow.*

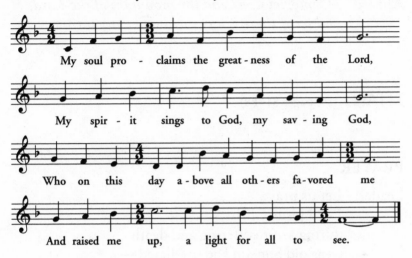

My soul pro - claims the great - ness of the Lord,

My spir - it sings to God, my sav - ing God,

Who on this day a - bove all oth - ers fa - vored me

And raised me up, a light for all to see.

Through me great deeds will God make manifest,
And all the earth will come to call me blest.
Unbounded love and mercy sure will I proclaim
For all who know and praise God's holy name.

God's mighty arm, protector of the just,
Will guard the weak and raise them from the dust.
But mighty kings will swiftly fall from thrones corrupt.
The strong brought low, the lowly lifted up.

Soon will the poor and hungry of the earth
Be richly blest, be given greater worth.
And Israel, as once foretold to Abraham,
Will live in peace throughout the promised land.

All glory be to God, Creator blest,
To Jesus Christ, God's love made manifest,
And to the Holy Spirit, gentle Comforter,
All glory be, both now and evermore. Amen.

All: *~Come, let us ascend the mountain of the Lord,
and see if there is any sorrow like my sorrow.*

LITANY (see pages 84–88)

PRAYER

Leader: Let us pray:
Lord Jesus Christ,
during your suffering and death
—as old Simeon had predicted—
a sword of sorrow pierced the heart
of your Mother.
As we reverently meditate on her sorrows,
may we reap the happy fruit of your passion.
You live and reign, now and for ever.

All: *~Amen.*

NOVENA PRAYER

Leader: Holy Mother of God and Queen of Heaven,

All: *~At Tepeyac you promised to show
all the nations of the earth
your love, compassion, help, and protection.*

Because you are our merciful mother,
hear our laments, and remedy all our miseries,
        misfortunes, and sorrows.
Stamp your priceless image on our hearts,
unveil your precious will for us,
and hold us in the hollow of your mantle
where you cross your arms,
now and always and for ever and ever.
Amen.

BLESSING

Leader: May Our Lady of Compassion,
        standing at the foot of the Cross,
        + obtain for us true sorrow for all our sins.

All: *~Amen.*

THE SEVENTH DAY:
MARY IN THE UPPER ROOM

At the beginning of Luke's gospel and in the first chapter of its continuation, the Acts of the Apostles, Mary makes two prominent appearances: First, when the angel of the annunciation proclaims the incarnation and she willingly accepts the overshadowing of the Holy Spirit (Luke 1:26–38); second, when, after the ascension, she gathers with the apostles in the upper room and devotes herself to prayer with them while they await the promised descent of the Spirit (Acts 1:12–14). Although the second chapter of Acts does not explicitly mention her presence at the Pentecost event, her absence is inconceivable. Just as she was present at the Savior's birth, she is present at the birth of the church. She is the first of his disciples in virtue of her humble submission to God's call at the first descent of the Holy Spirit; she is first among the disciples and apostles at the second descent of the Spirit; she is named "Queen of the Apostles and Mother of the church." The mystery of her continuing presence and intercession in and for the church is, in a very special sense, apparent in the encounter of Saint Juan Diego and Our Lady of Tepeyac.

THE SPIRITUAL MOTHER
OF THE CHRISTIAN COMMUNITY

The disciple whom Jesus loved can say of Mary that she is the Mother of Jesus and also his own mother; he realizes then the intimacy which unites him with Christ, his Lord and his Brother. Mary, the Mother of Jesus and his mother, is the person who is able to draw him closer to Christ, his Lord and his God. With him she has been the witness of the last moments of the crucifixion, she has heard the last words of Jesus, and has received the Spirit which he has transmitted to the Church. Mary is therefore for him, and, through him, for all the disciples and for the Church which gathers about them, a very close sign of the presence of the Lord, a spiritual mother in the Christian community, the most venerated of all the spiritual mothers found in the Church, the spiritual mother par excellence of the beloved and faithful disciple, of the brothers of Jesus, which every Christian is called to be.

—Max Thurian of Taizé, 1920–1996

CALL TO PRAYER

Leader: Blessed be the great Mother of God,
Mary most holy!

All: *~She was overshadowed by the Holy Spirit!*

Leader: The daughter of the king is clothed with splendor, alleluia!

All: *~Her robes are embroidered with pearls
set in gold, alleluia!*

HYMN

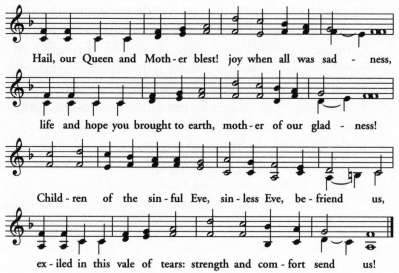

Hail, our Queen and Moth-er blest! joy when all was sad - ness,

life and hope you brought to earth, moth-er of our glad - ness!

Child - ren of the sin - ful Eve, sin - less Eve, be - friend us,

ex - iled in this vale of tears: strength and com - fort send us!

Pray for us, O Patroness,
Be our consolation!
Lead us home to see your Son,
Jesus, our salvation!
Gracious are you, full of grace,
Loving as none other,
Joy of heaven and joy of earth,
Mary, God's own Mother!

READING (Choose one of the following.)

In Prayer
Acts 1:12–14

[After the ascension] the apostles returned to Jerusalem from
the mount called Olivet, which is near Jerusalem, a sabbath

Text: *Salve Regina*, tr. James Quinn, SJ. Text © James Quinn, SJ. Selah Publishing Co. Inc., North American agent,
www.selahpub.com

day's journey away. When they had entered the city, they went to the room upstairs, where they were staying, Peter, and John, and James, and Andrew, Philip and Thomas, Bartholomew and Matthew, James son of Alphaeus, and Simon the Zealot, and Judas son of James. All these were constantly devoting themselves to prayer, together with certain women, including Mary, the mother of Jesus, as well as his brothers.

SILENCE

RESPONSE

Leader: Stay here in the city, alleluia!

All: *~Until you have been clothed with power from on high, alleluia!*

(Or this)

FILLED WITH THE HOLY SPIRIT
ACTS 2:1–4

When the day of Pentecost had come, they were all together in one place. And suddenly from heaven there came a sound like the rush of a violent wind, and it filled the entire house where they were sitting. Divided tongues, as of fire, appeared among them, and a tongue rested on each of them. All of them were filled with the Holy Spirit and began to speak in other languages, as the Spirit gave them ability.

SILENCE

RESPONSE

Leader: The Holy Spirit will come upon you, O Mary, alleluia!

All: *~And the power of the Most High will overshadow you, alleluia!*

CANTICLE OF THE BLESSED VIRGIN MARY
LUKE 1:46–55

Leader: Come, Holy Spirit,

All: *~Fill the hearts of the faithful and kindle in them the fire of your divine love, alleluia!*

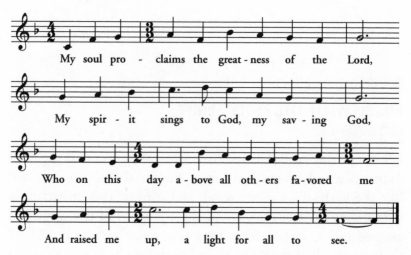

My soul pro - claims the great - ness of the Lord,

My spir - it sings to God, my sav - ing God,

Who on this day a - bove all oth - ers fa - vored me

And raised me up, a light for all to see.

Through me great deeds will God make manifest,
And all the earth will come to call me blest.
Unbounded love and mercy sure will I proclaim
For all who know and praise God's holy name.

God's mighty arm, protector of the just,
Will guard the weak and raise them from the dust.
But mighty kings will swiftly fall from thrones corrupt.
The strong brought low, the lowly lifted up.

Soon will the poor and hungry of the earth
Be richly blest, be given greater worth.
And Israel, as once foretold to Abraham,
Will live in peace throughout the promised land.

All glory be to God, Creator blest,
To Jesus Christ, God's love made manifest,
And to the Holy Spirit, gentle Comforter,
All glory be, both now and evermore. Amen.

All: *~Come, Holy Spirit,*
        fill the hearts of the faithful
        and kindle in them the fire of your divine love,
        alleluia!

LITANY (see pages 84–88)

PRAYER

Leader: Let us pray:
         Lord our God,
         you desired that the Mother of your Son

should be present and joined in prayer
with the first Christian community.
Grant us the grace
to persevere with her in awaiting the Spirit,
that we may be one in heart and mind
and come to taste
the sweet and enduring fruits of redemption.

We ask this through our Lord Jesus Christ,
    your Son,
who lives and reigns with you and the Holy Spirit,
one God, for ever and ever.

All: *~Amen.*

NOVENA PRAYER

Leader: Holy Mother of God and Queen of Heaven,

All: *~At Tepeyac you promised to show*
            all the nations of the earth your
            love, compassion, help, and protection.
            Because you are our merciful mother,
            hear our laments, and remedy all our miseries,
                misfortunes, and sorrows.
            Stamp your priceless image on our hearts,
            unveil your precious will for us,
            and hold us in the hollow of your mantle
            where you cross your arms,
            now and always and for ever and ever.
            Amen.

BLESSING

Leader: May the great Mother of God, Mary most holy,
the Queen of Apostles and Evangelists,
+ be our unceasing intercessor
before the throne of God.

All: ~*Amen.*

THE EIGHTH DAY: THE FALLING ASLEEP IN DEATH, THE ASSUMPTION, AND THE CORONATION OF MARY AS QUEEN OF HEAVEN

This ancient feast of the falling asleep in death and of the bodily assumption of the Virgin Mary is observed on the dedication day of one of the first churches erected in her honor in Jerusalem in the fifth century. It was introduced into the Roman liturgy around the middle of the seventh century. In Jerusalem, Rome, and Constantinople, great civic processions were held in her honor on this day, and in many countries it became a kind of early harvest festival when churches were strewn with herbs and flowers to mark the occasion. On November 1, 1950, Pope Pius XII defined this venerable article of faith as a dogma.

Like her Son, Mary is life-out-of-death, the loving Mother of all those who believe and strive for what we confess in the Apostle's Creed: "the resurrection of the body and life everlasting."

THE ASSUMPTION

To the temple of the Lord not made by hands there today has come to rest Mary, a holy tabernacle, re-enlivened by the living God. David, her father, rejoices, and with him choirs of Angels and Archangels; choirs of Virtues and of Principalities are glorifying her; choirs of Powers and of Dominations and of Thrones sing exultingly to her; the Cherubim and the Seraphim

---

praising chant her glory. For today the immaculate Virgin, undefiled by earthly affection, whose nourishment was heavenly thoughts, returns not again to the world with re-enlivened body, but is assumed into the tabernacles of heaven. How could that one taste death from whom the true life flowed out to all? Yet she did fall under the law inflicted by him whom she bore, and as a daughter of the old Adam she suffered the old sentence of death, even as her Son who is life itself. But now as Mother of the living God, she is fittingly taken up to heaven by Him. For how could death feed on this truly blessed one who had eagerly listened to the word of God? who at the Archangel's salutation, filled with the Holy Spirit, conceived the Son of God? who without pain gave birth to Him? whose whole being was ever consecrated to her Creator? Could hell receive such a one? Could corruption destroy a body in which Life had been brought forth? For her a way is prepared to heaven—a way that is straight and fair and easy. For if Christ, the way and the truth, has said: "Where I am there also shall My servant be," does it not follow that His Mother is surely with Him?

—*Saint John of Damascus, ca. 675–749*

CALL TO PRAYER

Leader: Blessed be the great Mother of God,
            Mary most holy!

All: *~Daughter of Jerusalem, you are beauty itself,*

Leader: Serene as the moon, as bright as the dawn,

All: *~And dazzling like the sun!*

HYMN

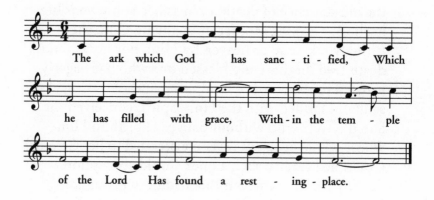

The ark which God has sanc - ti - fied, Which
he has filled with grace, With - in the tem - ple
of the Lord Has found a rest - ing - place.

More glorious than the seraphim,
This ark of love divine;
Corruption could not blemish her
Whom death could not confine.

God-bearing Mother, virgin chaste,
Who shines in heaven's sight,
She wears a royal crown of stars
Who is the door of light.

To Father, Son, and Spirit blest
May we give endless praise
With Mary, who is queen of heaven,
Through everlasting days.

READING (Choose one of the following.)

VICTORY OVER DEATH
1 CORINTHIANS 15:52–57

The trumpet will sound, and the dead will be raised imperishable, and we will be changed. For this perishable body must put on imperishability, and this mortal body must put on immortality. . . . Then the saying that is written will be fulfilled:

"Death has been swallowed up in victory."
"Where, O death, is your victory?
Where, O death, is your sting?"

The sting of death is sin, and the power of sin is the law. But thanks be to God, who gives us the victory through our Lord Jesus Christ.

SILENCE

RESPONSE

Leader: As angel choirs rejoice, alleluia!

All: *~Mary is taken up into heaven, alleluia!*

(Or this)

BLESSED AMONG WOMEN
LUKE 1:41–45

Elizabeth was filled with the Holy Spirit and exclaimed with
a loud cry, "Blessed are you among women, and blessed is
the fruit of your womb. And why has this happened to me,
that the mother of my Lord comes to me? For as soon as
I heard the sound of your greeting, the child in my womb
leaped for joy. And blessed is she who believed that there
would be a fulfillment of what was spoken to her by the
Lord."

SILENCE

RESPONSE

Leader: The Queen stands, O Lord, at your right hand,
alleluia!

All: ~*Arrayed in vestments of gold, alleluia!*

CANTICLE OF THE BLESSED VIRGIN MARY
LUKE 1:46–55

Leader: A great portent appeared in heaven:

All: ~*A woman clothed with the sun,*
with the moon under her feet,
and on her head a crown of twelve stars.

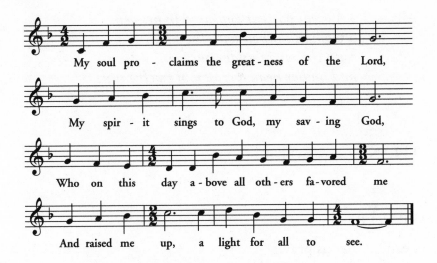

My soul pro - claims the great-ness of the Lord,
My spir - it sings to God, my sav - ing God,
Who on this day a - bove all oth - ers fa-vored me
And raised me up, a light for all to see.

Through me great deeds will God make manifest,
And all the earth will come to call me blest.
Unbounded love and mercy sure will I proclaim
For all who know and praise God's holy name.

God's mighty arm, protector of the just,
Will guard the weak and raise them from the dust.
But mighty kings will swiftly fall from thrones corrupt.
The strong brought low, the lowly lifted up.

Soon will the poor and hungry of the earth
Be richly blest, be given greater worth.
And Israel, as once foretold to Abraham,
Will live in peace throughout the promised land.

All glory be to God, Creator blest,
To Jesus Christ, God's love made manifest,
And to the Holy Spirit, gentle Comforter,
All glory be, both now and evermore. Amen.

All: *~A great portent appeared in heaven:*
         a woman clothed with the sun,
         with the moon under her feet,
         and on her head a crown of twelve stars.

LITANY (see pages 84–88)

PRAYER

Leader: Let us pray:
         Almighty God,
         you gave a humble virgin
         the privilege of becoming the mother of your Son,
         and crowned her with the glory of heaven.
         May the prayers of the Virgin Mary
         bring us to the salvation of Christ
         and raise us up to eternal life.
         We ask this through our Lord Jesus Christ,
              your Son,
         who lives and reigns with you and the Holy Spirit,
         one God, for ever and ever.

All: *~Amen.*

NOVENA PRAYER

Leader: Holy Mother of God and Queen of Heaven,

All: *~At Tepeyac you promised to show*
         all the nations of the earth
         your love, compassion, help, and protection.

Because you are our merciful mother,
hear our laments, and remedy all our miseries,
  misfortunes, and sorrows.
Stamp your priceless image on our hearts,
unveil your precious will for us,
and hold us in the hollow of your mantle
where you cross your arms,
now and always and for ever and ever.
Amen.

BLESSING

Leader: May the great Mother of God, Mary most holy,
the queen of all saints,
+ intercede for us with the Lord.

All: *~Amen.*

THE NINTH DAY:
OUR LADY OF GUADALUPE

The more I try to comprehend the intrinsic force and energy of the apparitions of Our Lady of Guadalupe to Juan Diego in Tepeyac in 1531, at the beginning of the Americas, the more I dare to say that I do not know of any other event since Pentecost that has had such a revolutionary, profound, lasting, far-reaching, healing, and liberating impact on Christianity.

—Virgilio Elizondo

MOUNT TEPEYAC, SACRED MOUNTAIN

Mount Tepeyac takes its place among the famous mountains of God's saving history. It is the Mount Sinai of the Americas, for it is here that God gives the new law of love, protection, and compassion for the people. It is the Mount of the Beatitudes of the Americas, for through the relationship and conversation between the Lady and Juan Diego, we can hear and experience a blessing pronounced on the poor, the meek, the lowly, the sorrowing, the peacemakers, and the persecuted of the new world. It is the Mountain of the Transfiguration of the Americas, for here the glory of God is clearly manifested to God's chosen one, Juan Diego. It is the Americas' version of the mountain from which the resurrected Lord commissioned the apostles to go forth and make disciples of all nations (Matthew 28:16), for it is here that Juan Diego is commissioned to go and request a common home for "all

the inhabitants of these lands." It is indeed God's
sacred mountain of the Americas.

—*Virgilio Elizondo*

CALL TO PRAYER

Leader: Blessed be the great Mother of God,
Mary most holy!

All: *~Blessed be our Lady of Guadalupe,
Mother of the Americas!*

Leader: O Mary, you are more worthy of honor
than the cherubim

All: *~And far more glorious than the seraphim.*

HYMN

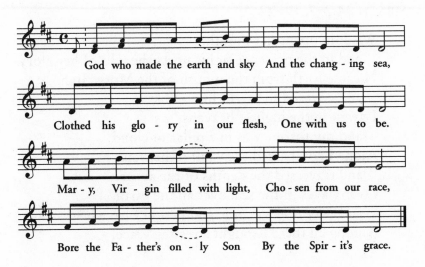

God who made the earth and sky And the chang - ing sea,

Clothed his glo - ry in our flesh, One with us to be.

Mar - y, Vir - gin filled with light, Cho - sen from our race,

Bore the Fa - ther's on - ly Son By the Spir - it's grace.

Mary, Virgin filled with light,
Chosen from our race,
Bore the Father's only Son
By the Spirit's grace.

He whom nothing can contain,
No one can compel,
Bound his timeless Godhead here,
In our time to dwell.

God, our Father, Lord of days,
And his only Son,
With the Holy Spirit praise:
Trinity in One.

READING (Choose one of the following.)

OUR LADY OF WISDOM
SIRACH 24:2–7, 19–22

Wisdom opens her mouth,
    and in the presence of his hosts she tells of her glory.
"I came forth from the mouth of the Most High,
    and covered the earth like a mist.
I dwelt in the highest heavens,
    and my throne was in a pillar of cloud.
Alone I compassed the vault of heaven
    and traversed the depths of the abyss.
Over waves of the sea, over all the earth,
    and over every people and nation I have held sway.
Among all these I sought a resting place.

Come to me, you who desire me,
    and eat your fill of my fruits.
For the memory of me is sweeter than honey,
    and the possession of me sweeter than the
      honeycomb.
Those who eat of me will hunger for more,
    and those who drink of me will thirst for more.
Whoever obeys me will not be put to shame,
    and those who work with me will not sin."

SILENCE

RESPONSE

Leader: Blessed is the womb that bore you, O Christ,
           alleluia!

All: *~And the breasts that nursed you, alleluia!*

(Or this)

THE NICAN MOPOHUA, 23–25

"I am the Ever-Virgin Holy Mary, Mother of the God of Great Truth, Teotl, of the One through Whom We Live, the Creator of Persons, the Owner of What is Near and Together, of the Lord of Heaven and Earth.

"I very much want and ardently desire that my hermitage be erected in this place. In it I will show and give to all people all my love, my compassion, my help, and my protection because I am your merciful mother and the mother of all the nations that live on this earth who would love me, and who would place their confidence in me. There I will hear their laments and remedy and cure all their miseries, misfortunes, and sorrows."

SILENCE

RESPONSE

Leader: Blessed are you among women, O Virgin Mary,

All: *~And blessed is the fruit of your womb, Jesus.*

CANTICLE OF THE BLESSED VIRGIN MARY
LUKE 1:46–55

Leader: We turn to you for protection,

All: *~Holy Mother of God.*
         Listen to our prayers
         and help us in our needs.
         Save us from every danger,
         glorious and blessed Virgin.

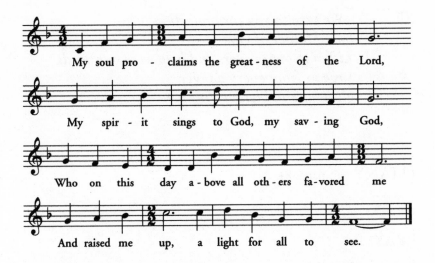

My soul pro - claims the great-ness of the Lord,
My spir - it sings to God, my sav - ing God,
Who on this day a - bove all oth - ers fa - vored me
And raised me up, a light for all to see.

Through me great deeds will God make manifest,
And all the earth will come to call me blest.
Unbounded love and mercy sure will I proclaim
For all who know and praise God's holy name.

God's mighty arm, protector of the just,
Will guard the weak and raise them from the dust.
But mighty kings will swiftly fall from thrones corrupt.
The strong brought low, the lowly lifted up.

Soon will the poor and hungry of the earth
Be richly blest, be given greater worth.
And Israel, as once foretold to Abraham,
Will live in peace throughout the promised land.

All glory be to God, Creator blest,
To Jesus Christ, God's love made manifest,
And to the Holy Spirit, gentle Comforter,
All glory be, both now and evermore. Amen.

All: ~We turn to you for protection,
      holy Mother of God.
      Listen to our prayers and help us in our needs.
      Save us from every danger,
      glorious and blessed Virgin.

LITANY (see pages 84–88)

PRAYER

Leader: Let us pray:
         God of power and mercy,
         you blessed the Americas at Tepeyac
         with the presence of the Virgin Mary of Guadalupe.
         May her prayers help all men and women
         to accept each other as brothers and sisters.

         Through your justice present in our hearts
         may social justice and peace reign in the world.

         We ask this through our Lord Jesus Christ,
             your Son,
         who lives and reigns with you and the Holy Spirit,
         one God, for ever and ever.

All: ~Amen.

NOVENA PRAYER

Leader: Holy Mother of God and Queen of Heaven,

All: *~At Tepeyac you promised to show*
         all the nations of the earth
         your love, compassion, help, and protection.
         Because you are our merciful mother,
         hear our laments, and remedy all our miseries,
         *   misfortunes, and sorrows.*
         Stamp your priceless image on our hearts,
         unveil your precious will for us,
         and hold us in the hollow of your mantle
         where you cross your arms,
         now and always and for ever and ever.
         Amen.

BLESSING

Leader: May Mary of Guadalupe,
         the precious Mother of God,
         the One who cares for everyone,
         + be our comfort and our joy.

All: *~Amen.*

LITANY

Leader: Lord, have mercy

All: ~*Lord, have mercy*

Christ, have mercy

~*Christ have mercy*

Lord, have mercy

~*Lord, have mercy*

God our Father in heaven

~*have mercy on us*

God the Son, Redeemer of the world

~*have mercy on us*

God the Holy Spirit

~*have mercy on us*

Holy Trinity, one God

~*have mercy on us*

Holy Mary

~*pray for us*

Holy Mother of God

~*pray for us*

Most honored of virgins

~*pray for us*

Mother of Christ

~*pray for us*

Mother of the church

~*pray for us*

Mother of divine
grace

~*pray for us*

Mother most pure

~*pray for us*

Mother of chaste
love

~*pray for us*

Mother and virgin

~*pray for us*

Sinless Mother

~*pray for us*

Dearest of
mothers,

~*pray for us*

Model of
motherhood

~*pray for us*

Mother of good
counsel

~*pray for us*

Mother of our
Creator

~*pray for us*

Mother of our
Savior

~*pray for us*

Virgin most wise

~*pray for us*

Virgin rightly
praised

~*pray for us*

Virgin rightly
renowned

~*pray for us*

Virgin most
powerful

~*pray for us*

Virgin gentle in
mercy

~*pray for us*

Faithful Virgin

~pray for us

Mirror of justice

~pray for us

Throne of wisdom

~pray for us

Cause of our joy

~pray for us

Shrine of the Spirit

~pray for us

Glory of Israel

~pray for us

Vessel of selfless
devotion

~pray for us

Mystical Rose

~pray for us

Tower of David

~pray for us

Tower of ivory

~pray for us

House of gold

~pray for us

Ark of the
covenant

~pray for us

Gate of heaven

~pray for us

Morning Star

~pray for us

Health of the sick

~pray for us

Refuge of sinners

~pray for us

Comfort of the
troubled

~pray for us

Help of Christians

~pray for us

Queen of angels

~pray for us

Queen of
patriarchs and
prophets

~pray for us

Queen of apostles
and martyrs

~pray for us

Queen of
confessors and
virgins

~pray for us

Queen of all saints

~pray for us

Queen conceived
in grace

~pray for us

Queen raised up to
glory

~pray for us

Queen of the
rosary

~pray for us

Queen of peace

~pray for us

Saint Juan
Diego, poor
campesino

~pray for us

SPONTANEOUS PRAYERS OF INTERCESSION

Lamb of God, you take away the sins of the world

~have mercy on us

Lamb of God, you take away the sins of the world

~have mercy on us

Lamb of God, you take away the sins of the world

~have mercy on us

Pray for us, holy Mother of God.

~That we may become worthy of the promises of Christ. Amen.

(Return to the corresponding page of the day and continue with the prayer.)

Acknowledgments Continued

Reference on p. 3: Virgil Elizondo, *Guadalupe: Mother of the New Creation.* Maryknoll, New York: Orbis Books, 1998, 139 pages.

We turn, p. 9: The English translation "We turn to you for protection" from *A Book of Prayers* © 1982, International Committee on English in the Liturgy, Inc. All rights reserved.

The much desired feast, pp. 15–16: From a homily in *The Short Breviary.* Collegeville, Minnesota: The Liturgical Press, 1954, pp. 655–656.

Hymn, p. 17, Text: *The Stanbrook Abbey Hymnal,* © Stanbrook Abbey Press, 1974 and 1995. Music: POLSLOE, Mode 7:D.

Father of mercy, p. 21, Father, source, p. 35, Almighty God, p. 74, God of power, p. 82: Excerpts from the English translation of *The Roman Missal* © 1973, International Committee on English in the Liturgy, Inc. (ICEL). All rights reserved.

He who, pp. 23–24: Homily 5, 17 on the Nativity tr. by Thomas Buffer in Luigi Gambero, *Mary and the Fathers of the Church.* San Francisco: Ignatius Press, 1999, pp. 251–252. Reprinted with permission of Ignatius Press, San Francisco, CA.

Hymn, pp. 24–25, Text: Quem terra, pontus, aethera; Venatius Fortunatus, c530–609; Tr. John M. Neale, 1818–1866, alt. Music: EISENBACH, John H. Schein, 1586–1630.

Today is, p. 27: Byzantine troparion, translated by the author.

The word was, pp. 30–31: in *The Mary Book* by Frank Sheed. London: Sheed and Ward, 1950, p. 245. Sheed & Ward is an imprint of The Rowan & Littlefield Publishing Group, Lanham, MD.

Hymn, pp. 31–32, Music: WOODLANDS, Walter Greatorex, (1877–1949), © Oxford University Press. Used by permission. All rights reserved. Photocopying this copyright material is ILLEGAL.

I saw part, pp. 37–38: Excerpts from JULIAN OF NORWICH: *Showings,* translated from the critical text with an introduction by Edmund Colledge, OSA, and James Walsh, SJ, from The Classics of Western Spirituality, Copyright © 1978 by Paulist Press, Inc., New York/Mahwah, N.J. Used with permission of Paulist Press. *www.paulistpress.com*

Hymn, p. 39, Text: The Community of the Holy Name, © 1995 in *Hymns for Prayer and Praise,* The Canterbury Press. Music: *CREATOR ALME SIDERUM,* Plainsong, Mode IV.

Lord Jesus, p. 43, Abba, Dear father, p. 51, Lord Jesus, p. 58: composed by the author.

Christ's first, p. 46: from *The Life of Jesus* by François Mauriac. New York: David McKay, 1937, p. 28.

Hymn, pp. 47–48, Text: Roland Ford Palmer (1891–1895) © Estate of Roland F. Palmer. Music: PLEADING SAVIOR, *Christian Iste,* 1830.

Mary, the mother, pp. 53–54: Epistle 25 to the Church of Vercelli in *Brevarium Romanum,* Editio XX Iuxta Typicam, Pars Autumnalis. Ratisbonze: Friderici Pustet, 1943, pp. 508–509, translated by the author.

Hymn, p. 55, Music: *ERHALT UNS HERR,* Klug's *Geistliche Lieder,* 1543.

The disciple whom, pp. 60–61: From *Mary, the Mother of All Christians.* New York: Herder and Herder, 1964, p. 170.

Hymn, p. 62, Music: AVE VIRGO VIRGINUM (GAUDEAMUS PARITER), John Horn, 1544.

Lord, our God, p.66; God of power, p. 82: Excerpts from *Book of Mary* Copyright © 1987 United States Conference of Catholic Bishops, Inc. Washington, DC. Used with permission. All rights reserved.

To the temple, pp. 68–69: From *The Short Breviary* Collegeville, Minnesota: The Liturgical Press, 1954, pp. 637–638.

Hymn, p. 70, Text: *The Stanbrook Abbey Hymnal,* © Stanbrook Abbey Press, 1974 and 1995. Music: LAND OF REST, American.

The more, p. 76; Mount Tepeyac, pp. 76–77; I am, p. 79–80: From *Guadalupe: Mother of the New Creation* by Virgilio Elizondo. Maryknoll, New York: Orbis Books, 1998, pp. xi; 47–48; 8.

Hymn, pp. 77–78, Text: *The Stanbrook Abbey Hymnal,* © Stanbrook Abbey Press, 1974 and 1995. Music: ADORO TE DEVOTE; Mode V.

Litany, pp. 84–87: The English translation of the Litany of Loreto from *A Book of Prayers,* © 1982, ICEL. All rights reserved.